Not This Tender

Not This Tender

poems by
Sarah Uheida

Not This Tender

Dryad Press (Pty) Ltd
Postnet Suite 281, Private Bag X16, Constantia, 7848,
Cape Town, South Africa
www.dryadpress.co.za / business@dryadpress.co.za

Copyright © poems Sarah Uheida
All rights reserved

No part of this book may be reproduced or transmitted in any form or by any electronic or mechanical means, including photocopying and recording, or any other information storage or retrieval system, without prior written permission from the publisher or copyright holder.

Cover design & typography: Stephen Symons
Copy Editor: Helena Janisch
Cover Image: Nymphaeum in Sabratha, Libya
Set in 9.5/14pt Palatino Linotype
First published in Cape Town by Dryad Press (Pty) Ltd, 2025

ISBN 978-1-0370-4465-6 (Print)
ISBN 978-1-0370-4466-3 (Electronic)

Visit www.dryadpress.co.za to read more about all our books and to buy them. You will also find features, links to author interviews and news of author events. Follow our social media platforms on Instagram and Facebook to be the first to hear about our new releases.

Dryad Press is supported by the Government of South Africa through the National Arts Council of South Africa (an agency of the Department of Arts & Culture), whose assistance is gratefully acknowledged.

*In the house of someone who has been hanged,
do not speak of rope*
—Libyan proverb

CONTENTS

The First Night

Ribs of Satin, Mouth of Dusk	3
Forethought of Grief	6
If	7
Our Russian Holiday—I	8
If You Ever Knew Thirst, It Was When You Loved the Body Still	9
A Wound Cauterised in Light	10
What to Keep	12
And What You Leave Behind	13
Imagine Wars, Imagine Bodiless Women	14
Her Word Against Early Morning Light	15
Grief and I Want It	18

The First Pang

The Name of Home Dies Softly	23
The Inflamed Hour	24
17 May 2011	25
Hours	26
Waiting on a Word	27
Our Russian Holiday—II	28
De Kelders	32
A Grammar of Absence	33
Scab	34
Ruined by Tomorrow and the Fruit of Yesterday	35

The First Touch

And I Do It Beautifully	41
Portrait Sundays	42
Entering a Room	44
Home Is You and I	46
While It's Still Warm	47
You Lavish Berber Bitch	48
A Fig for Every Absence	50
If Waiting Is a Bargain You Make with the Gone	51
You are me and I am what happens when	54
The Sting Arrives Late	55
Overstay Appeal	56
Epilogue	59
Acknowledgements	61
Notes on Poems and Quotations	63

The First Night

Ribs of Satin, Mouth of Dusk

I
Father, Persephone's pomegranates fell from my mouth
when I came asking for the ease you once promised,
and you said, *the music that played then paralyses now.*

II
I, too, have turned feral, teeth on teeth.
You, too, sipped Cyrene's wine straight from dusk's
collarbone.

III
At the entrance of what was once my birthplace,
you sat threadbare, mourning the quiet of abandoned beds.
You said, *the sea still smooths the stone, knowing it remembers
the storm.*

IV
I needled through the days, bones bracing
for a famine yet to come.
How your hands glistened, Father,
when I spoke of sin.

V
The injustice of pen on paper,
the imperfect poetics of English on my tongue:
I never saw a wild thing sorry for itself.

VI
Father's mosaiced litanies, the way he raised me—
like hands to the sky—
undo every attempt at not-repenting.

VII
Rivers of *oh no*, of *Father no longer father*,
just another man
who could not love my fading away.

VIII
For after all, what is a daughter
but a splinter, a hereditary haemorrhage?

IX
And Allah, that coaxer of crude confessions,
as distant as the first time I forgave myself—
drank, and drunk on my innocence,
gathered husks of Jannah like seashells.

X
There was that one time, though,
when you taught me to spell *Mediterranean*,
and I asked if inheriting your religion
meant I could no longer bask in Berber myth.

XI
You said I still could.

XII
Father, how did you not notice the teething?

XIII
And there was that other time,
when I laid an offering at your feet, whisper-yelled:
let me be your debutante,
I'll let you hold my body like a grudge.

XIV
Be still, you said,
the prayer that played then paralyses now.

Forethought of Grief

Forgive this perfect day, its skies blued,
bruising earth's clavicle.
First there was dust and dirt and now: field,
the warm green pulse on the wrist of everything—

grasslands of gasps gathered and hidden
from ourselves, always dying,
to save something for later.
Extinction soaks my sleeve, I do not trade time

for air, living each hour till living hurts.
In the kitchen peeling pomegranates,
hoping hunger can teach me something;
forgetting straightaway.

Giving way in your eyes are days, days, days,
pour them like paint over poems you have
no home for, or bury them like warm prey
under the weight of tomorrow's hunt.

If

If you could powder this wound with me,

I'd ask you to start right here—

inside the poem, where I die on my own terms.

I die making up the soft, baby smell of your neck,

trying to render it all beautiful as if

you were going to be here for it.

I couldn't keep you, but let me bear your bruise

until we drain my body of the blood

that would have been yours.

Our Russian Holiday—I

This good body of mine is monthly skinned,
its mother an unfailing moonbeam
in the everywhere of night.

I had no problem shoving red-ruined
lingerie at the bottom of the trashcan,
but you loved digging it up; grinning,
you'd ask if the blood is blood.

Not even the trashcan is safe
from your foresight, ancient hands
gloved and rummaging for proof
of something mine, a loss we
could still skirt: are you looking for me
or my ruin?

You answer—*save for the body,
everything is salvageable*—
all you need is a bit of bleach;
pour it in the cheap sink 'til lace is
transparent and rosewater runs clear.

Then came my night of the haemorrhage.
I didn't know you soaked and scrubbed
while I slept high and hoping
the morning spares one of us.

Mother, if you sift through the wreckage,
what won't you keep? Come morning,
you'll uncurtain the house, barge in—

If You Ever Knew Thirst, It Was When You Loved the Body Still

This morning, burn your best candles and rewild the world. Tonight, you must put everything back exactly where you found it. Do not pull her out after a fall thirty metres deep or double as dark. Often when hurt, the wild horse leaves the herd behind to heal. If she dies, the raptors will circle her resting place. But if she lives, lord, she will outfly the hawks home to Fisherhaven, haul the whole moon across the displeasures of day. Ask her if surviving the fall feels like the first night coming home, her hoofbeats and hunger darkening the rivers as though a flood. And her, exquisite, and almost mended, a living creature that does not demand *wound* from every day galloping toward her. Or is it a snare-gash in an abandoned barn, split with sun, hard to want or hobble to—body, untouched, finding neither the refuge of night, nor another's sunshade?

A Wound Cauterised in Light

The days we slash and stay,
how the body never quite
writhes itself free
from blister and bruise,
catches in the skin of every doubt.
Some memories are so porous with pain
we would rather let them slice again,
renew our *here-and-now*,
aching like that first night,
when the blood takes precedence —
the red and warmth of it;
the sincerity in suffering
for someone else.

How we picnicked in the panic,
anaesthetised, smiling, finally even
each holding the other closed,
careful not to touch the wound.

Back then, before we knew what we were doing,
the body still sore to the touch, unscarred —
and, before the first time we'll undress just to brag,
compare how deep the cuts, how *forever*,
time having not started scabbing over.

And then last night,
needing to lose something,
how I unstitched it all,
on the dirty dinner table,
the hold of old bandages,
the itch of grief;

and all that I'd withheld
I hurled at you, all the hurt I could
or hoped to find,
and how for a second
everything held.

This is your poem:
thread and needle
are in the blue drawer.
Take what you need—
leave when you must.

What to Keep

The spine—gathered in a soft towel,
crated into some half-light, waiting
to wither or wound and weep—
has never known winter.

These brittle gestures: a child's drawing
before she learns the edge of things,
half-folded on the greasy counter,
unsentimental.

Teach her to waste the years
already no good; and do it now,
while time still has not begun
looking for her.

And What You Leave Behind

At twenty-six, I am still that same plagued child,
stuck between synonyms and sentences, suspended between
two countries neither of which would claim a woman
this distracted, this pedantic, this wide-eyed. I am on my knees,

sifting through the parallel intensities of things: *tenderness*
sounds softer in English, slides like silk on the tongue; but
the Libyan equivalent—*grief grinds my liver when I think of you*—
chafes, doesn't it? Monstrous. Marvellous. It burns and burns,

leaves a gutted gentleness, the kind you might learn to love if
you're desperate enough. In every poem, I hide the little girl.
In the best ones she sounds nothing like herself. Resonance,
dissonance—it doesn't matter, she devours all. She's mad

on jasmine. Eats it for dinner, leaves fruit out by the trashcans,
for no one. I teach her a thousand ways to write *Do you
understand me? Can you love me? Watch how pretty the poem is,
how it dresses itself, its satin dress. Satan. Distress. Kiss me. Kill me.*

Who cares. I missed Grandpa's calls. I miss Grandpa's calls.

Imagine Wars, Imagine Bodiless Women

She spilled the wine,
said, *let something darken us*;
reached for the ammunition I keep under the bed
for when the night negates our dreams
and I have to blow up something tangible.
With her hand on the back of my neck,
I will call someone who cares, only to hang up,
hurry across plains in a maroon dress I borrowed,
wear in case of war.
Too righteous to run, we throw our heads back,
take a last spoonful of bourbon
under a moon of bullets.
I crawl; she steps on my dress,
the field is a cigarette half lit.
She *says, I left too much behind*
so I shrug her off
like a winter sunset;
underwhelming, uncalled for,
she retreats; bravery
lowers the stakes;
love has always sheltered us
but I never did find a reason to stay—
only my explosive nature,
only this poem's implications.
Bent on breakage,
I trudge on, jasmine falling from my mouth
till I reach the other side,
turn around,
make my way back under a sulphide sky
more leisurely this time.

Her Word Against Early Morning Light

I
Single housekey—communal, cutthroat,
final as flowers that flowered.
Look: skies blue then blacken,
and they learn just how much one can do without.

II
The first time they viewed the property,
the tenant wasn't home.
They sat in her garden for a minute
and made up their minds.

III
She knows every flower's name from print alone,
poems underlined and words dog-eared,
yet cannot name a trembling thing.
Can't place a single touch-me-not, curling from itself,
not the panicgrass, the lace aloe, the rose-gold grasses.

And then there is the waiting green,
an unnamed bush that may or may not
unspool into roses.
She only came to see the garden.
Or, if she's feeling a little luminous
and not so pressed for time,
to put palm to soil and say: *grow*.

IV
No orange or fig tree here—
just rental lavender,
and for their bodies, a place to sleep.

V
While he does the paperwork, she busies herself
bruising petals, shears the old mattress, wilderness
escapee goes missing for a few minutes,
flees like leaves at night—returns with soap, incense,
candle, and a bit of flower food, and they perfume
their house with *you're-here-now*.

VI
For one last attempt at building something that keeps,
he will buy a new calendar in April,
glue the first three months together,
give up summer,
either way, a wreckage of the days
that dragged dreams they drew like breath
through the dirt she came from.

VII
Give her a tenderness worth the queues
and she'll confess she overstayed—
their laugh unfading, her floral heart,
his voice the only country she'd die for.

VIII
Where did the time go?

IX
She has learned silence now:
the less she talks about exile,
the more sure-footed their plans.

X
In the seconds before he wakes her—
the high of almost saying *stay*,
he thinks, *maybe tomorrow?*
His fears clawing at her back,
her word against early morning light.

XI
Wading through a decade of winters
she has spent in his country (she is spent in his country),
the trash bins each Tuesday, loadshedding schedules.
They have never missed rent,
even gave up watching the news.

XII
They've dodged the daybreak as best they could,
buried her passport, drank nothing
but rooibos honey—
he finally cracks:
never loveless, you and I, but—
oh, my love,
if these were roses,
they would have bloomed by now.

Grief and I Want It

The distance between here and my country
         is a fence of stunning nothings—
   tread it like qur'anic verses, string it with wedding lights,
      here—hang from it this loss

The First Pang

The Name of Home Dies Softly

I don't recall Arabic,
only lush lilac vowel and vein,
a skyful of synonyms for sunset
tangled in the mulberry tree.

Sometimes I'm like the ram
the night before Eid Al-Adah—
less noose than freedom.

The Inflamed Hour

You stun,
the small muscles of your hand
soft as scalpel.
And I am all artery today.
Hear how time, that expectant pause, is loud as blood—
as if the hour, self-conscious about its beautiful borders,
insists we slice it open.

17 May 2011

We all learn to eat our grief
in pieces, paraphrasing home.

When you leave, do it like a man
in love with war, or a little boy
naming his country.

Your grandmother stands, framed
by the arched doorway, her expression eclipsed.
Through stained glass, she spits:
A worthy woman knows when to let the dying die—
and unbolts the gate for you.

Hours

Morning arrives,
salted butter pancakes, a little rain;
a mound of cinnamon spilled
onto the last bite.

Someone laughs, how timeless.

Waiting on a Word

The phone call every Eid: my first word is a tumour in the throat,
the eye reddens before your voice arrives.
I want to beg someone for something.

You ask if I need money.
You ask what I'm studying.
You ask: what am I studying?

You grow older, and thinner,
and less you. And I can't explain expired papers,
though I know they told you I didn't try hard enough.

I waste your wisdom, throw your words around like confetti—

they whiten

grow grey

then

absence.

Our Russian Holiday — II

You barged in with a glass of orange
juice, early — time still on your side —
scanning the room for my sobs,
the forgive-me you were sure
had to be there, somewhere.

I did not lie.
You didn't know what to do
with all your motherly mercy,
bundled on your lap like clean clothes.

I didn't ask you
to scrub the cold red clots
or change the sheets so we forget —
I just sat, combing my hair.

But you had to dig me up,
brushed brittle strands,
tucked a stubborn knot behind my ear.
This body was splinter,
and your kindness broke my spine.

The small animal I was —
I would have given up anything —
the poetry, the smoking, the mourning —
just to tell you something died here.

But you pulled my hair so bloody hard,
I learnt silence is absolution,
and confessing was just a selfish daughter
begging for the love she fucked away.

You yanked the hair you'd spent
all morning unknotting, had a way
of making any ache feel well-deserved,
and I understood.

A mother can always tell
the innocence of a skinned knee
from a suffering summoned, knows
blood from wound, from birth, from love.

But a daughter scavenges,
digs it all up, red and cruel
and split-end, all in the name
of this little poem. She is me —

and I ruin the image of you, pained, pale
on that plastic chair —
the night you laboured alone,
body battling birth and death.

Four rounds of anaesthesia
and one daughter to show for it.
Hair blood-wet, thinning before your eyes —
you struck me, screeched
I don't want to see your face right now
you howled and heaved.

But all your howls taught me
was that a daughter shall hoard everything —
memory, mistake, miracle, and word —
this is how we heal our mothers.

You, gutted lamb, unthreadable,
as I stood intact and smiling
till my lip split—

and for just a second,
in that ugly hospital room,
all pain belonged to you.

They said the foetus was too small to bury,
but never let you see how small.
I was never going to tell you
something died here.

*

Mother, years ago, when the nurses sent *you* home
empty-handed—uterus no longer womb,
in the car, you asked, almost forgiven—
When can we visit the grave?

He switched off the engine, said nothing.
In his cold carcass car, we could've given up anything,
anyone, for a word from him.

But silence folded you into his backseat,
precise as a needle—you stuffed your body
into the silhouette of the driver's seat:
this is the first time you disappear.

Beside you, the can of baby-blue paint
you'll eventually give away.
And Daddy, not looking at me
is how I teach myself to replace you.

Our tinned family felt lighter now—
two kilograms apart,
your face a little thinner,
his ten years older—
nothing left to want.

Two cigarettes later, he said,
No, we can't visit.
We won't find the gravestone.
The coffin's empty, he added.
While you lay losing his son,
his car was broken into—
the baby bag is gone.

And anyway, he sang,
like everything was sun—
Why cut through snow and sinew
when you can sob just as well at home?

De Kelders

~ Gansbaai, Western Cape

A tremor will only know the world tremoring,
      stirring the days with impossible tenderness,
           that it unwraps and wraps around the heart.

A Grammar of Absence

At first, I save a little money, keep every scrap of sightseeing, and every splinter from the *here and now*: poem and wound alike; degree, debris, dirge. I press them into crisp dictionary pages to read you, but the waiting gets too long, not a year or two, and the story goes stale and harder for us to hear. I lose most of my Arabic to the waiting. I lose the rest the moment I stop forcing myself to forget.

A moment before the dictionary pages mildew, I taste my nature: I am a terrible granddaughter. Pathetic with need, dismisser of spilled blood, wasteful woman whining that she's still worthy. Did you ever tell me I was not? I want to save the woven cover, but I have to save myself first. You expect too much of me—a call, a visit, announcing a child or a marriage or a miscarriage, blaming someone for something, anything that'll excuse the absence.

I save my tears, unshed, salt unspent, and go home to the poem I wrote you in a language you could not understand. I sleep inside words you will never mouth, never mispronounce. I do not save enough money to cross the distance. I do not save enough money to cross you. You've died and I am still comparing metaphors. So close to finding the right words the ones that say what you want to hear and I don't know what you want to hear and now you can't hear me and I need you to hear me so I can ask, *did you miss me, what do you want me to say, granddad,* and tell you what I need to tell you as soon as I find the right words and soon I'll find the right words.

Scab

It's nightfall, and night falls—
and no sky is untouchable.
The world is fabric and flesh,
and we feel it tearing, a crevice
of luminous unrest you try to hide from me.

The cat crawls behind the couch,
the washing machine breaks again.

Ruined by Tomorrow and the Fruit of Yesterday

I
Do not fear fantasies
—feral, fevered, fatal as they are—
your body, a casualty of *come closer*.
If I break your rib in contrition,
if the sky scuttles past this lightless want,
will your mouth still famish mine?

II
I read of olive picking—
how costly this greenness
that does not yield softly to the crush.
Sixty-six million trees line the land in silence.
Do you know Bshaaleh's ancient roots?
Six millennia of olive wood in Lebanon,
witnesses, biblical and sanctified,
saddened by our fading flesh.

III
And I remember how
you said you ate only one colour.
But was it the unripe green
or the bruised black?
Will you tell me some things again,
fill my mouth with first-time-ness?
Will you remind me often and blamelessly
of the *whys* of this love?

IV
The first time the tree lost itself to ground,
stood dressed in centuries to come, it said:
You cannot claim you've lost your way
when I've already shown
what I want,
where I'll stay.

V
It comforts me to think
that past this—past our bodies—
there will be something rooted somewhere,
something that must've watched us be,
a living thing that frames: look,
they were here. And here. And here.

VI
To sleep beside someone
is to sedate every instinct,
to renounce disappearing.
To risk each artery again and again.
So, imagine the enormity of my promise
each time you trust me with your sleeping body.
Why I cannot afford night—
not with a heart's weight on my right shoulder,
the serrated knives of all that isn't us,
and the soft scalpels of your hand
always unfurling,
never letting go.

VII
It breaks me
to say your name
and hear nothing back.

VIII
The olive tree never asks for rain,
but my god, will it kneel and drink.

The First Touch

And I Do It Beautifully

For every burial I miss, I sing a poem. I excavate a language of vacant words, rinse it in rosewater, press it flat and clean as the silence that splits mother from father. They drink their tea without speaking, and my heart does not break for them. They heal in their crooked way, but they heal. Meanwhile, my words and I disfigure each other, breathless, barking. Language foams at the mouth. Behind my back, these lungs, cunning, starving, pocket a little air each time I open my mouth. I make your death about me.

Portrait Sundays

Seep into your oversized t-shirts, yesterday's wine stains
mingling in the laundry basket. You rest, you *sun*, you
won't let the moon's name dismantle the afternoon.

On your throne of books, a modern Cleopatra,
you stuff each void with its own absence, let the small lives
cease their shuffling, allow everything to become.
& it feels good.

You take yourself honey-tasting, slow the sweetness down
—hibiscus, eucalyptus, wildflower—
no need for pacing, no need for bracing,
file your nails and teeth, brew rosemary into something
prehistoric, unnamed.

You set no traps for wolves, bolt no doors.
There's no need for cages, now your body is no longer a
waiting room. & it feels good to walk away from the Lost-
and-Found mouths of men, extracting yourself like peach
skin caught between their teeth, emerging whole, to bask in
the shade of a cold cup of coffee.

You've learned how to shop for watermelons,
ask for a taste now, before carrying the heavy pinkness
of love across the uncalled for. & this is no metaphor:
you went to the library, read everything there is about fruit.

Now you wring the blandness of forced affection from
your hair, let it fall, strand by strand, into a night river.
& it feels good.

You unfasten the weight of what was never yours,
strip it off like old skin, pockets purpled with mulberry,
skyful of here-and-now, by yourself for yourself—
fluent in the dialect of your own quiet,
unthreading the faultline between aloneness and ease,
no witness, but the slow-lit thrum of your loosening ribs.

Entering a Room

The poem is deceptive—
we are not the children of tomorrow,
so do not break my jaw with spring and summer,
with ponds and pearls.
I saw you sitting in a puddle of survivor's guilt,
and I walked right past.
I've got my own rivers to drink dry.
All I wanted was shelter for the night;
hold me cowardly, that I may wake and walk.
My bed was set on fire thirteen years ago,
and now, touch me where there is already blood—
touch like burn and bandage.
Look what I've done with this room
I have charred the walls,
smoked your perfume out of the pillows.

Oh, and honey, I won't be able to make the dinner date,
or breakfast in bed. Cannot get back—
got caught in the details, in the open fire,
caught stealing bread, breaking my affection
against your wishes, whispering to the enemy,
or in the bombs of 2011,
a boy's body, a match lit,
another woman, bodiless.

There's this saying in Libyan—
how does it go, oh god?
I'm trying to detangle memory from trauma,
to open backdoors to my childhood,
so as not to have the alarms impale me.

Entering a room is not the same as exiting it—
that's how it went.
Entering a room is not the same as exiting it,
and you have been entering and entering,
so sinless.

Look at the mess I've made:
each poem I give you is a papercut
that seems insipid;
the blood just doesn't gush, goddamn it.

Out of a scab, I write a ballad,
bleed Sabratha dry out of boredom.
You hide my history from me,
lasso the pages like gillnets.
I think of the Mediterranean and its depravities,
lapping at my mouth;
I think of the Roman ruins on which Mama built
us a house, and now—ruined ruins,
and now—revelation inside mirages.
To want you is to betray the war,
to change my mind after I've buried everyone
I swore I'd die before.
A wake—a waking up too gentle—
give me your mouth like a hook,
pass my panties,
I need to go back to my country,
for entering a room is not the same as exiting it,
and I have been exiting and exiting,
so sinless.

Home Is You and I

every time I tell someone we're Tripoli escapees I risk losing you to some far refugee prison where they'll never let us see each other again / oh, but you and I are so perfect / even like this, with less than we need / one closet one surname one word for war / and if I am the weaker daughter then help mother and father hide my body from me / how you owned a single nice dress and I burned it / bury this cigarette in their bed with me / I will protect you inside this burning house the way a blue flame saves a red flame from water /

home is you and I / daddy's detainees / his ember anger / we melt in it love him for it / open-palmed-we-greet-it / *thank you for the coals oh thank the warmth of your wrath / here we'll wrap it in expired passport paper* / but this weak mother of ours / god she'll wail about anything / he slapped me and she sobbed / he dirtied her days calling us *sluts* and she sobbed / severed my box of cigarettes in two / served me baklava in her best silverware / through the long nights of withdrawal, made me dormant / I was fever and shiver / I was vulgar as lung cancer / but you / sister / hand in cold hand / you helped me cross the borders safely / saved me / the way a red heart saves its bluing brain from oxygen

While It's Still Warm

Always the same plates,
the small insults sipping them dry.

The clang of fork and knife from
the neighbour's house—sharper than theirs.

Everything else is realer than this,
real family, real cutlery, real lives.

Even in a houseful of *ifs*
dinner is dinner is dinner,

night is always night,
and when they laugh,

it is in a language
they understand.

You Lavish Berber Bitch

And why not you,
king of poetics,
Moët & Chandon swallower,
wanting to mingle with the divine,
to fuck,
to lounge,
to make pesto from scratch.

At Lanzerac's Craven Lounge—
Lamia in designer tuxedo,
dark furniture eyes, mahogany
gaze, its curve and cave
kohled in rings of saffron,
ready to unsee the world.

Three fireplaces pillar the room,
a hearth for each version of your myth—
prophetess of want, devourer of children,
you faultless Eve.
Say *be* and it is.

Smoke bends into a bloodline
born and buried tonight;
nervous oaks hide the windows,
make excuses for all your excess.
All that is touched is ruined rawhide,
the sink of Yves Saint Laurent on your skin
amour & armour: a colonial send-off.

You, 1925 invader,
pleasurer of earth, you:

Perold's wife the night she leaves him,
bored of his dusty desk,
the racks of Pinot Noir & Cinsault.
Also you: the morning he begs her to come home,
placing the world's first bottled Pinotage at her feet,
say *quiver* and he is emptied—
you, ceremony and altar,
throatful of intrigue, poison oak,
Stellenbosch serpentine—
you sicken and cure, sip and spit,
scarcity in glassfuls,
a lifeform feeding by the riverbank.

And tonight:
you, Tripoli patriarch,
Mortal Queen of Ancient Libya,
the unbidden spectre
at each Keldermeester Versameling—
Zeus's Lamia haunting their vines,
souring the fruit with a single glance
whispering ruin into the barelled dark.

They'll tell on you,
invoke Heritage,
call upon their Heras—
you lavish Berber bitch, moonlit rot,
safekeeping half-lit Cuban cigars
under leather ottomans—
vanishing then returning with one
of your ninety-nine names:
despoiler, devourer, desirer, savourer, saviour—
sipping on their last good bottle of Pinotage.

A Fig for Every Absence

If I still deserve sweetness, then for every fig I eat, I must let one rot on the counter. That's the only way to miss you. Not in lack but in a waiting that feels unused.

It is not enough to never feast on fruit again. To forget the taste of sugar is to forget to miss it. No, I must spoon homesickness into my mouth and it must taste unsalvageable. It hasn't just been a year or two after all.

If Waiting Is a Bargain You Make with the Gone

A father's job is not to teach his children
to swim but to pull their bodies from the water
each time they are drunk by Tripoli's blue-blue-blue—
and this July heat, honest about its thistle and thirst.

He leaves them ashore, shoals where salt
clogs noses and is instantly forgiven,
their bones already memorising the stride
and stray of swaying water, for the dark hours—
when they will close their eyes
and still feel the sea's insistence
on the beauty of dreamless sleep.

Their dad plunges ahead, his body
softens the fall, and he smiles to himself,
weightless in Mediterranean melancholia.

He dives, drifting past the two orange flags
hung up by fishermen who know
rip current, bait, moon and tide—
men who can tell patience from waiting,
and know which one comes first.

(If waiting is a bargain you make with the gone
—hollowed with hope porous with promise selfish as
sacrifice and more brittle— then patience is how the sea will
say, *sorry for your loss*.)

But he looks back. He always looks back.
Neck straining for the yellow and pink
of their smallness, their shrill inland laughter

a deserted lighthouse that, unneeded
by men and unloved by water, sits brilliant
and blinking at itself, luminous for no one.

He never taught his daughters to swim,
though it was not a broken-winged bird thing,
was not a tyrant father thing; just sweet, blue-lipped
delirium, that he could always swim back in time
or if too far, unearth them later, undrown them,
these gilled girls of his: he keeps
forgetting to waterproof their lungs.

On that same searing morning,
blue-irised sky bored and light-blind,
one daughter learns waiting,
the other not-returning.

It isn't even 8 a.m.,
and the sun is starting to sing,
peeling dark shoulders, less scornful
more paled with pretty plight.

And July, like so much unfinished business,
comes up for air again and again.

But of course, he always swims back,
back just in time, of course
he saves them, loves them—
and the sea is spared, every sky
charcoaled and moonlit,
the cantaloup starred open,
sweetness soaking sleeves.

So much summer inertia,
a good night's sleep,
on beds he built
from sturdy teakwood;
and his children, who, full of safe landings,
forget all his leaving—unlearn patience—
until the next morning,
when they'll follow him back into the sea.

You are me and I am what happens when

everything is glitter; everything you touch with your beautiful, empty hands becomes history—ancient, purposeful, already past death. Your only preoccupation is the past; no yesterday is water under the bridge. Not unlike god, you dwell in the aftermath—the vacuum in your chest when the world says, *no*. Loss so lonely, you mistake it for everyone else. And you dine on excuses, so here: it was never yours to undo. The only lesson worth learning is how to do without forgiveness. Even you recognise, at the gleam of failure, aglow and unsparing, the unparalleled pleasures of days spent unwisely.

The Sting Arrives Late

You're under, and I am nursing these papercuts, thin skin too translucent to earn its sting. What is so terrible about dying, anyway? Not even Allah can still the same pulse twice. But I? I scavenge, sift through the wreckage, turn pockets inside out for specks of you. In this poem alone, I have managed to bury then exhume you a thousand times. Not even Allah.

Overstay Appeal

The following documents must be submitted:

1. Written representation.
2. A copy of the declaration of undesirability (form 19) issued at the Port of Entry.
3. A copy of the relevant pages of the passport, including biopage.
4. Acknowledgment of receipt (in cases where the applicant has applied for a permit and the status is still pending).
5. If the applicant overstayed due to medical reasons, a medical certificate must be submitted.

I have borrowed money from everyone I love.
I have thrown dinner parties.
I have wanted to go home.
I have wanted to stay.

I have wanted to be many things,
but not this tender.

Epilogue

"So refine distance with the competence of a skilled professional and not the vulnerability of a perplexed lover. The poetry of exile is not what exile says to you, but what you say to it, one rival to another. Exile, too, is hospitable to difference and harmony. So fashion yourself out of yourself. And do not forget to thank exile graciously: I will praise you O exile, where praise becomes you. There, under the fig tree that will welcome me, at my mother's house, a passerby in a passing autumn!"

— Mahmoud Darwish, *In the Presence of Absence*

Acknowledgements

Deep gratitude is offered to the editors of the journals and anthologies that first housed versions of some of these poems: *The Atlanta Review, the other side of hope, The Shore, Plume, Every Day Fiction, 14 Magazine, New Contrast* and *We Call to the Eye and the Night: Love Poems by Writers of Arab Heritage.*

I am also thankful to the Miles Morland Foundation for their generous support, which enabled me to dedicate time to writing. Originally awarded for my memoir-in-progress, their funding made this poetry collection possible in ways both direct and intangible.

And I am so grateful:

> to Michèle Betty who has guided me, not just as a poet, but as a woman finding her way—for belief that never wavered, for wisdom that met me exactly where I was, for mentorship that extended beyond poetry into something larger, something steady; for teaching me what it means to shape a book, to trust a voice, to carry both courage and clarity; for every kindness, spoken and unspoken; for being someone I could come to with anything;

> to Sally-Ann Murray, for fierce care, for faith, for poetry; for meeting every poem I brought to you with open hands; for the creative risks, the academic journey, the long conversations, the high standards you set and to which you made me rise;

> to my mother, father and two sisters, who held me through every silence, every departure, every return: we are home;
> to my faraway Libyan family, who surrounded me with so

much love that I am willing to wait in unbearable longing for another 15 years to return for a lifetime: I will see you soon; to my grandfather Abu-Ajela, to whom I never got to say goodbye, whose life was already a kind of poetry— for the elegance of his Arabic handwriting, the volumes of Nizar Qabbani, the journals he filled with stories of his travels, the cassettes of Fairuz spinning softly in the background, for a love for language I absorbed without realising; to my grandmother Mehdia—for the verses that pour from you without paper, without pen, for the quiet strength and intensity that found its way into me;

to Tyler, for introducing me to a love so vast I had to keep writing just to find the edges of it; for reading, for listening, for living every poem with me; for knowing when to pull me back into the world, when to place a hand in mine, when to let me breathe; for every poetry reading, every poem read aloud, every book you gifted me; for giving me all the space in the world without ever making me feel alone: you are language;

to my friends in South Africa who kept me here and built a home around me—for every book given, every conversation that carried us through, every moment of encouragement when I needed it most: you are a constant;

to the poets and writers who remind me why language is a place to live, to those who came before, those beside me, and those yet to arrive;

and to you, the reader—for making a home for these words, for meeting me here: may they offer you something quiet, something kind; may they soften your world, if only for a while.

– Sarah Uheida

Notes on Poems and Quotations

Phrases and quotations have been used, sometimes with and sometimes without acknowledgement.

Page 3

I never saw a wild thing sorry for itself.

—D. H. Lawrence, 'Self Pity' in Vivian de Solo Pinto and F. Warren Roberts (eds.), *The Complete Poems of D. H. Lawrence* (London: William Heinemann, 1964)

Page 25

The 17th of May 2011 is the day on which Sarah Uheida and her family left war-torn Libya and arrived in South Africa. She was 13 years of age and unable to speak English.

Page 59

So refine distance with the competence of a skilled professional and not the vulnerability of a perplexed lover. The poetry of exile is not what exile says to you, but what you say to it, one rival to another. Exile, too, is hospitable to difference and harmony. So fashion yourself out of yourself. And do not forget to thank exile graciously: I will praise you O exile, where praise becomes you. There, under the fig tree that will welcome me, at my mother's house, a passerby in a passing autumn!

—Mahmoud Darwish, *In the Presence of Absence* 6ed, translated by Sinan Antoon (United States: archipelago books, 1967), p. 85.

OTHER WORKS BY DRYAD PRESS

THE DRYAD PRESS LIVING POETS SERIES

earth-circuit, iyra e m maharaj
Night Transit, P. R. Anderson
Dark Horse, Michèle Betty
Star Reverse, Linda Ann Strang
Transcontinental Delay, Simon van Schalkwyk
The Mountain Behind the House, Kobus Moolman
In Praise of Hotel Rooms, Fiona Zerbst
catalien, Oliver Findlay Price
Allegories of the Everyday, Brian Walter
Otherwise Occupied, Sally Ann Murray
Landscapes of Light and Loss, Stephen Symons
An Unobtrusive Vice, Tony Ullyatt
A Private Audience, Beverly Rycroft
Metaphysical Balm, Michèle Betty

OTHER PUBLISHED WORKS

The Creative Arts: On Practice, Making & Meaning,
edited by Michèle Betty and Sally Ann Murray
Palimpsests, Chris Mann
River Willows: Senryū from Lockdown, Tony Ullyatt
missing, Beverly Rycroft
The Coroner's Wife: Poems in Translation, Joan Hambidge

Available in South Africa from better bookstores nationwide, online at www.dryadpress.co.za, and internationally from African Books Collective at www.africanbookscollective.com.

Sarah Uheida is a Libyan-born poet and essayist, living and working in Cape Town. She holds a BA Honours degree in English literature and a Master of Arts in English Studies (specialising in poetry) from Stellenbosch University, both with distinction. Her MA was funded following the award of a Margaret McNamara Education Grant. In 2021, Sarah was the recipient of the internationally renowned Miles Morland Foundation Writing Scholarship. She is also the recipient of the 2020 Dan Veach Prize for Young Poets, which invites poetry from college-age students across the United States and internationally. Sarah's poetry and lyric essays have been widely published, both locally and abroad, in anthologies like *We Call to the Eye & the Night* by Persea Books, and *Relations: An Anthology of African and Diaspora Voices* by HarperCollins, and in journals like *New Contrast*, *Atlanta Review*, *the other side of hope*, *The Shore*, *fresh.ink*, *Plume* and *Every Day Fiction*. She is a regular contributor at poetry reading groups such as Off the Wall and The Red Wheelbarrow. *Not This Tender* is her debut collection.

www.ingramcontent.com/pod-product-compliance
Lightning Source LLC
Chambersburg PA
CBHW051133160426

43195CB00014B/2462